HAL•LEONARD
BASS PLAY-ALONG
'80s METAL

VOL. 16

T0066121

ISBN 978-1-4234-1439-1

HAL•LEONARD®
CORPORATION

7777 W. BLUEMOUND RD. P.O. BOX 13819 MILWAUKEE, WI 53213

Visit Hal Leonard Online at
www.halleonard.com

CONTENTS

Bass Notation Legend

Bass music can be notated two different ways: on a *musical staff*, and in *tablature*

THE MUSICAL STAFF shows pitches and rhythms and is divided by bar lines into measures. Pitches are named after the first seven letters of the alphabet.

TABLATURE graphically represents the bass fingerboard. Each horizontal line represents a string, and each number represents a fret.

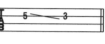

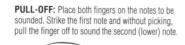

3rd string, open   2nd string, 2nd fret   1st & 2nd strings open, played together

HAMMER-ON: Strike the first (lower) note with one finger, then sound the higher note (on the same string) with another finger by fretting it without picking.

PULL-OFF: Place both fingers on the notes to be sounded. Strike the first note and without picking, pull the finger off to sound the second (lower) note.

LEGATO SLIDE: Strike the first note and then slide the same fret-hand finger up or down to the second note. The second note is not struck.

SHIFT SLIDE: Same as legato slide, except the second note is struck.

TRILL: Very rapidly alternate between the notes indicated by continuously hammering on and pulling off.

TREMOLO PICKING: The note is picked as rapidly and continuously as possible.

VIBRATO: The string is vibrated by rapidly bending and releasing the note with the fretting hand.

SHAKE: Using one finger, rapidly alternate between two notes on one string by sliding either a half-step above or below.

NATURAL HARMONIC: Strike the note while the fret hand lightly touches the string directly over the fret indicated.

MUFFLED STRINGS: A percussive sound is produced by laying the fret hand across the string(s) without depressing them and striking them with the pick hand.

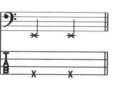

BEND: Strike the note and bend up the interval shown.

BEND AND RELEASE: Strike the note and bend up as indicated, then release back to the original note. Only the first note is struck.

RIGHT-HAND TAP: Hammer ("tap") the fret indicated with the "pick-hand" index or middle finger and pull off to the note fretted by the fret hand.

LEFT-HAND TAP: Hammer ("tap") the fret indicated with the "fret-hand" index or middle finger.

SLAP: Strike ("slap") string with right-hand thumb.

POP: Snap ("pop") string with right-hand index or middle finger.

Additional Musical Definitions

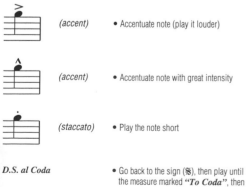

| | (accent) | • Accentuate note (play it louder) |

Fill — • Label used to identify a brief pattern which is to be inserted into the arrangement.

| | (accent) | • Accentuate note with great intensity |

• Repeat measures between signs.

| | (staccato) | • Play the note short |

D.S. al Coda — • Go back to the sign (𝄋), then play until the measure marked *"To Coda"*, then skip to the section labelled *"Coda."*

1. 2. — • When a repeated section has different endings, play the first ending only the first time and the second ending only the second time.

5

Big City Nights

Words and Music by Klaus Meine and Rudolf Schenker

1. When the day-

Verse

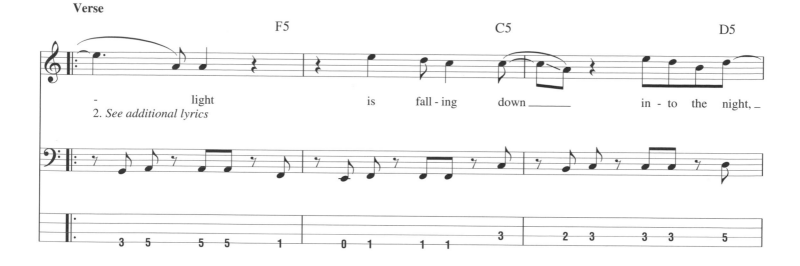

F5   C5   D5

\- light   is   fall-ing down _____   in - to the night, _

2. *See additional lyrics*

2nd time, substitute Fill 1

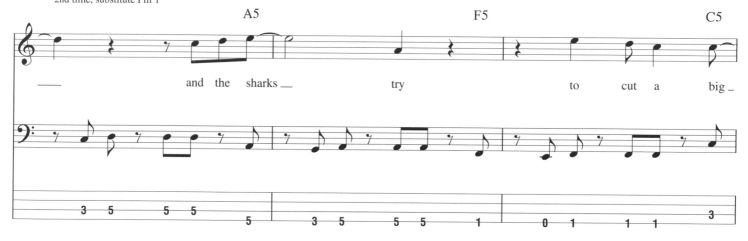

A5   F5   C5

___   and the sharks _   try   to cut a big _

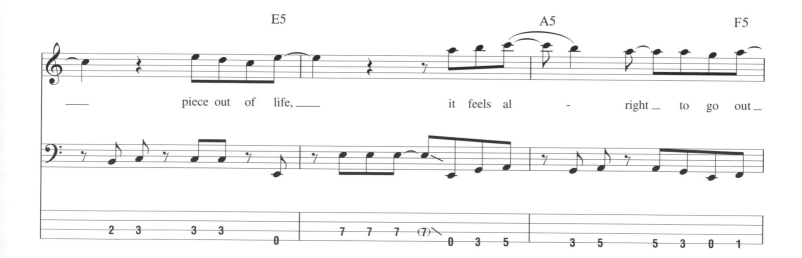

E5   A5   F5

___   piece out of life, ___   it feels al - right _ to go out _

Fill 1

10

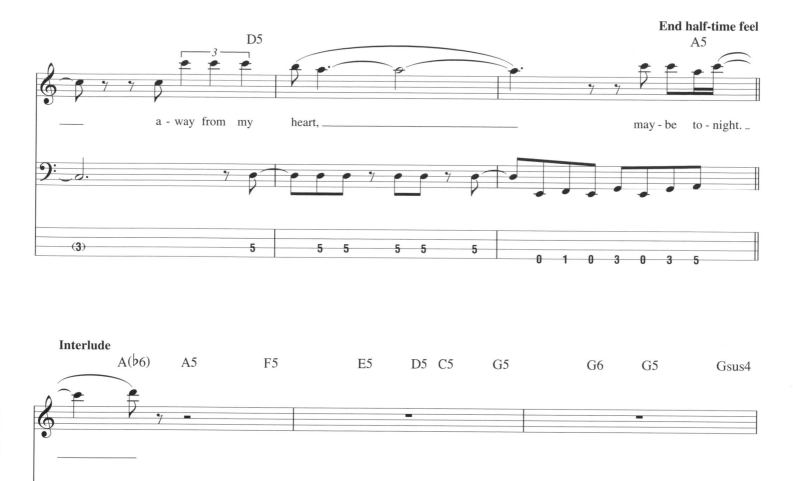

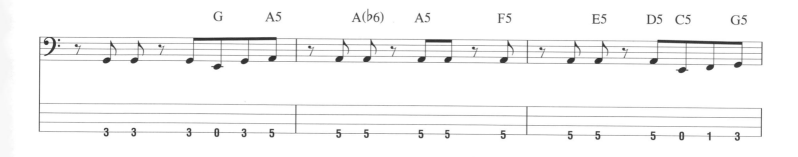

Outro-Chorus

Additional Lyrics

2. When the sunlight is rising up in my eyes,
   And the long night has left me back at somebody's side,
   It feels alright for a long sweet minute, like hours before.
   But it's more like looking out for something, can't find anymore.

(Bang Your Head)
Metal Health

Words and Music by Carlos Cavazo, Kevin Dubrow, Frankie Banali and Tony Cavazo

Intro
Moderate Rock ♩ = 118

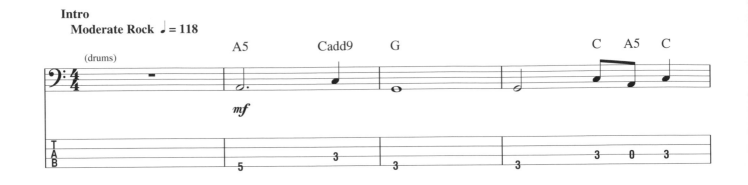

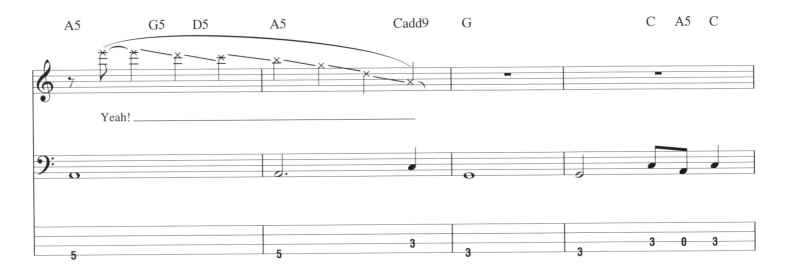

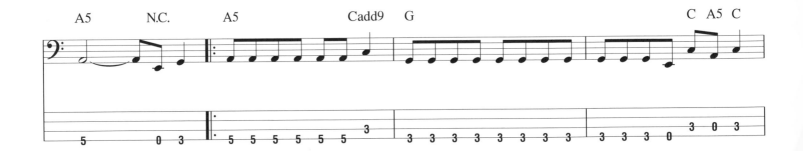

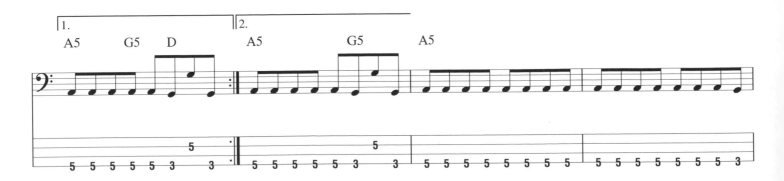

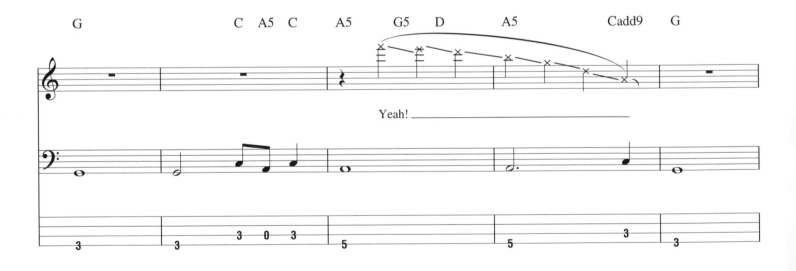

Yeah! _____

Ha, ha, ha, ha, ha, ha.

Rock Me

Words and Music by Alan Niven, Mark Kendall, Jack Russell and Michael Lardie

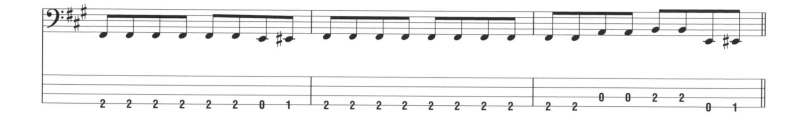

Verse

F#m

1. Sweet lit - tle ba - by, you don't have to go. _____

Lit - tle ba - by, tell me you won't go. _

Oh, we'd be so good to -

Play 3 times

Verse
F#m

2. Search the world _ for some - one I'll nev -

er find. _

Some-one who ain't, _ oo, _

_ the _ hurt - in' _____ kind. _

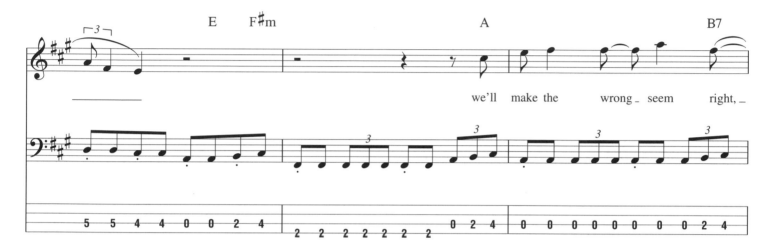

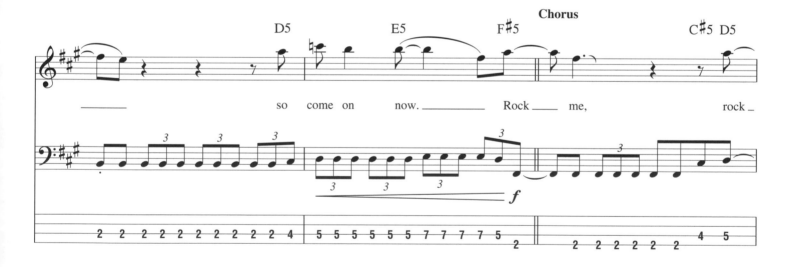

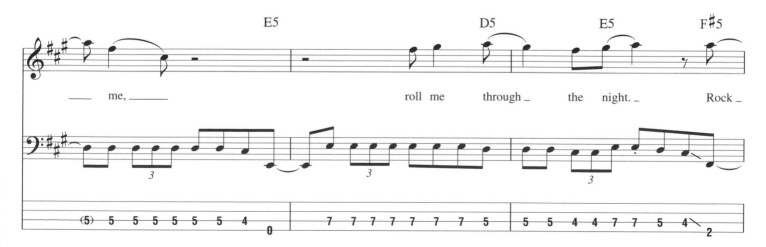

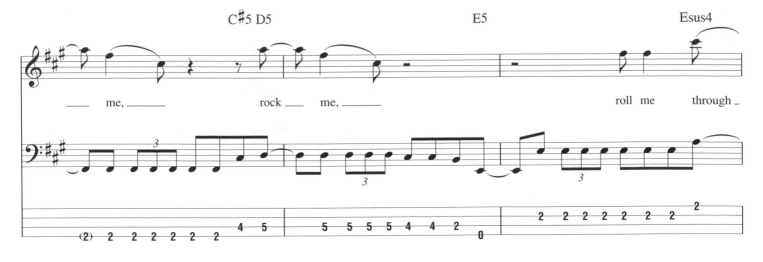

C#5 D5　　　　　　　　　　　E5　　　　　　　　　Esus4

me,　　　　rock　me,　　　　　　　　roll me　through

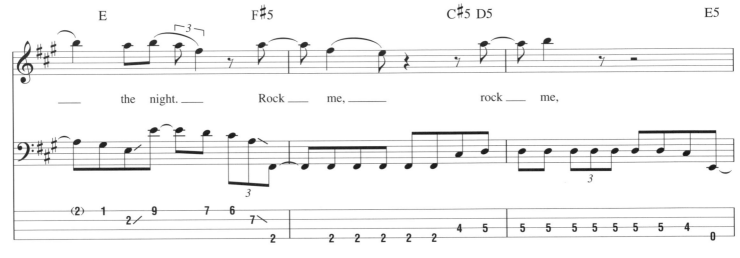

E　　　　　　F#5　　　　　　　C#5 D5　　　　　　E5

the night.　　Rock　me,　　　　　rock　me,

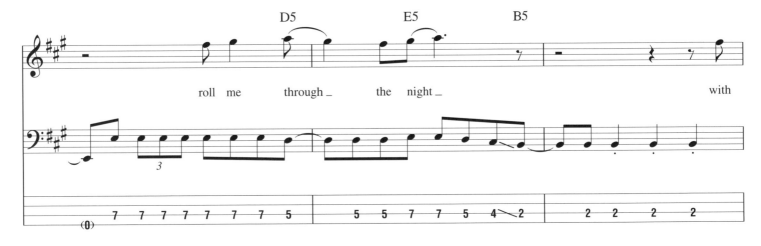

D5　　　　　E5　　　　B5

roll me　through　the night　　　　　　with

Interlude
F#m

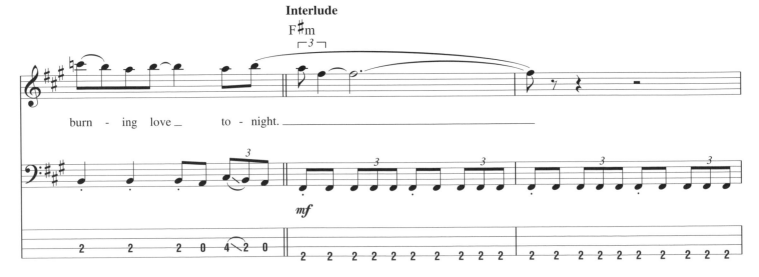

burn - ing love　to - night.

mf

30

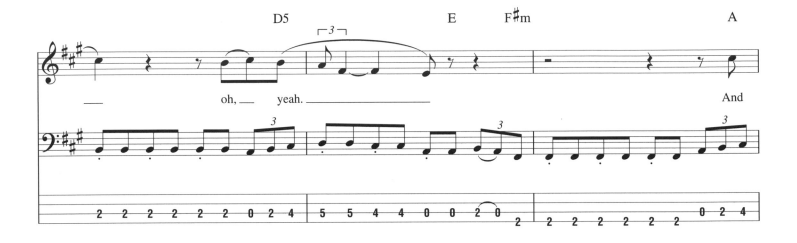

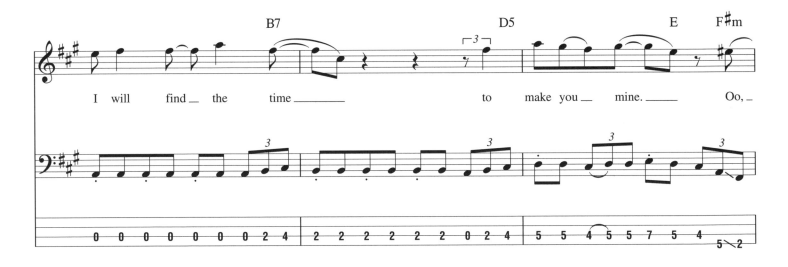

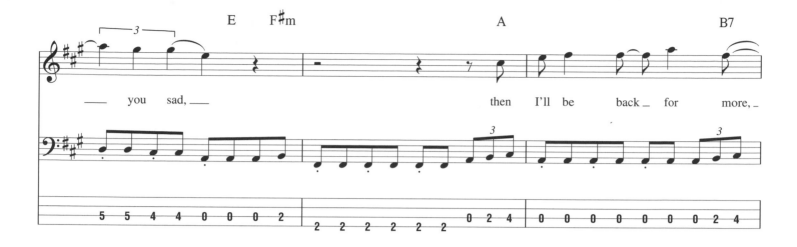

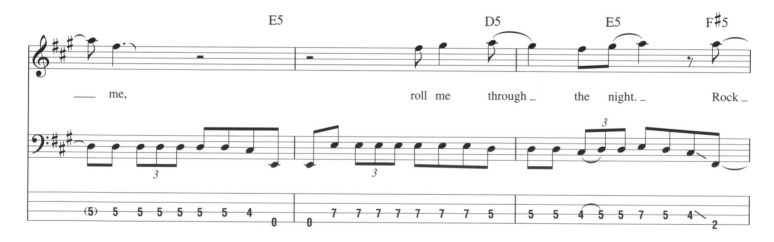

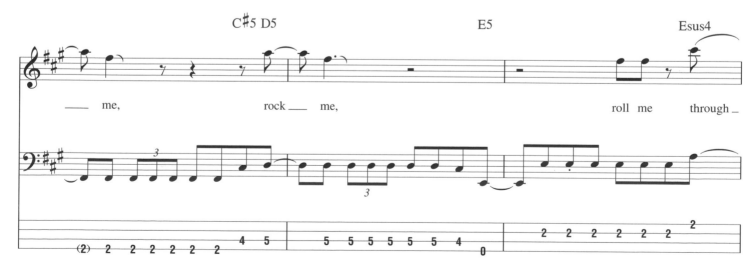

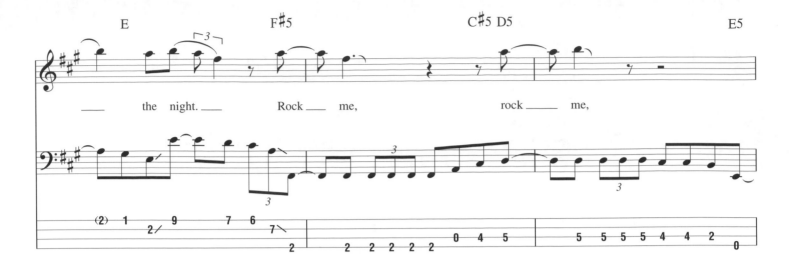

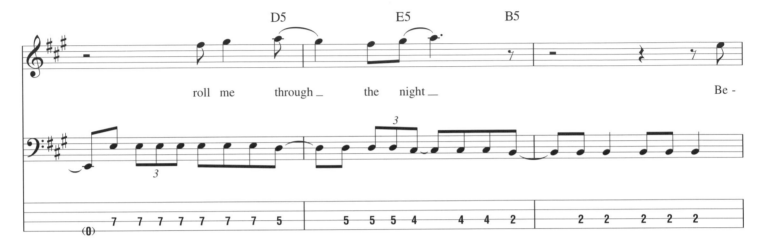

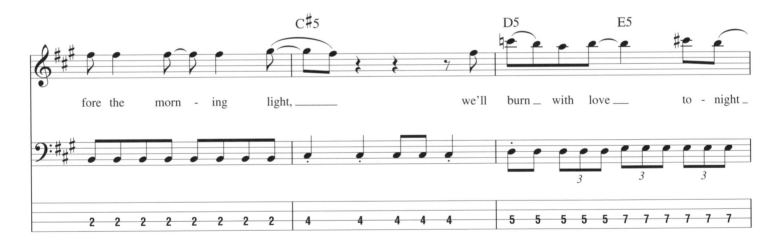

34

Guitar Solo

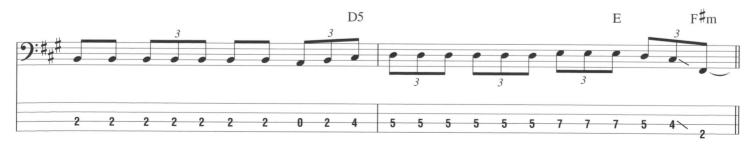

Verse

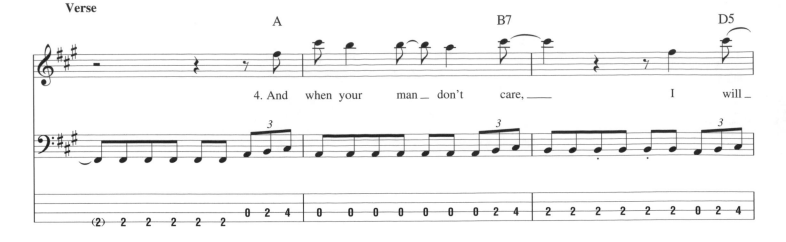

Chorus

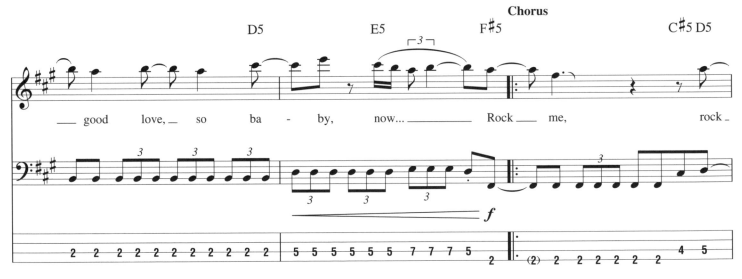

2nd time, substitute Fill 1

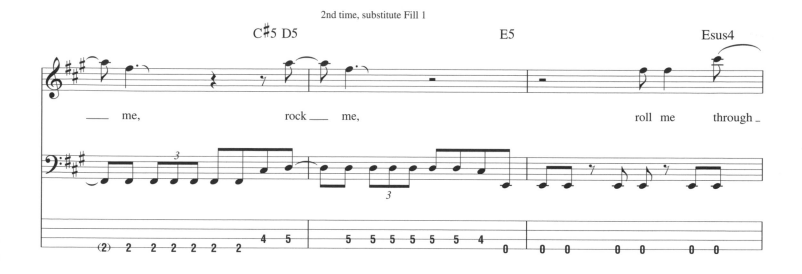

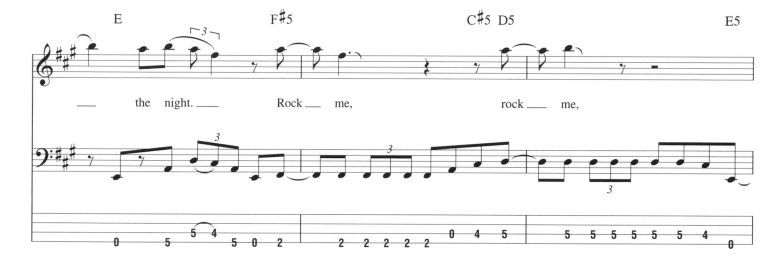

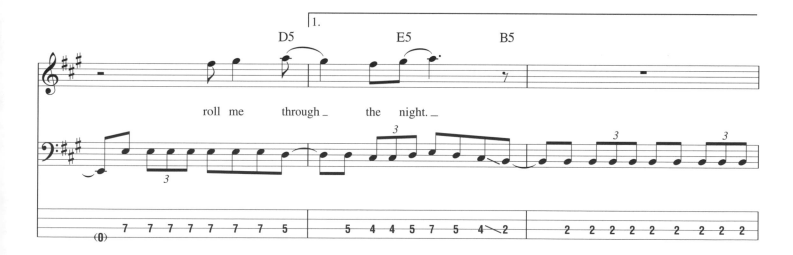

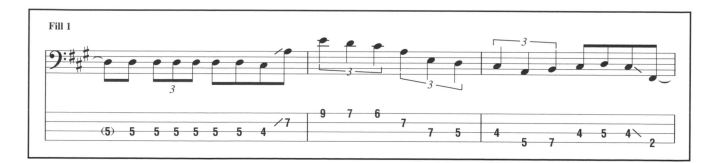

There's no wrong or right, we'll burn with love. Rock

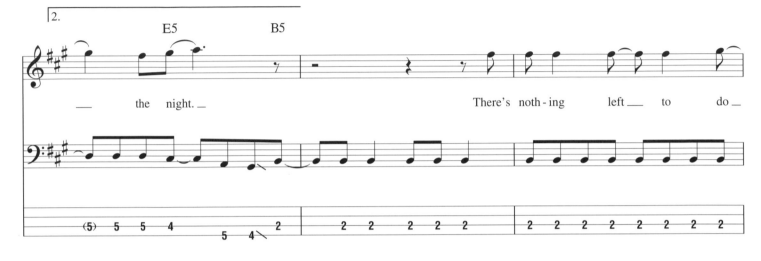

the night. There's noth-ing left to do

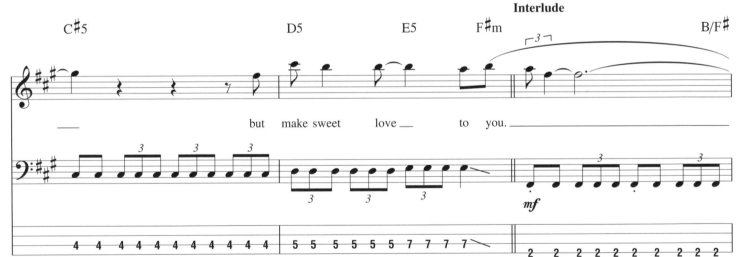

but make sweet love to you.

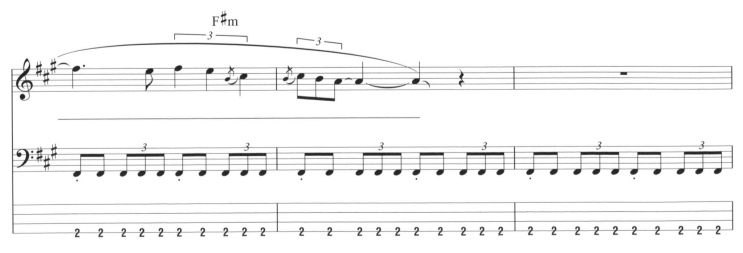

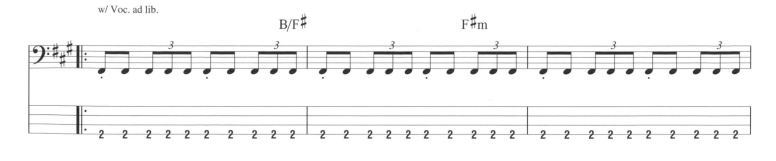

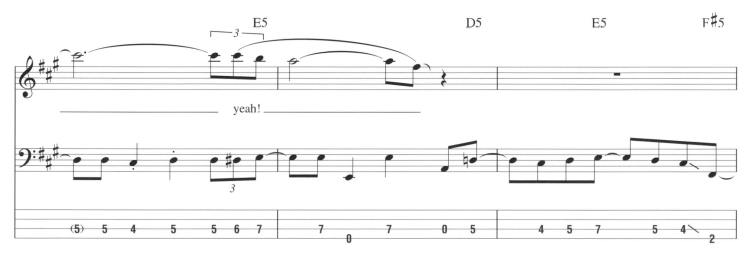

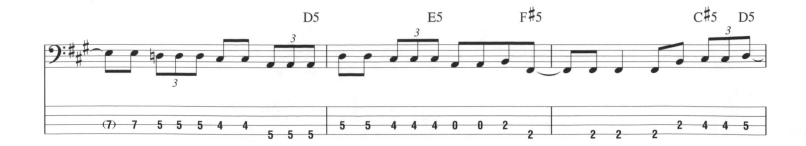

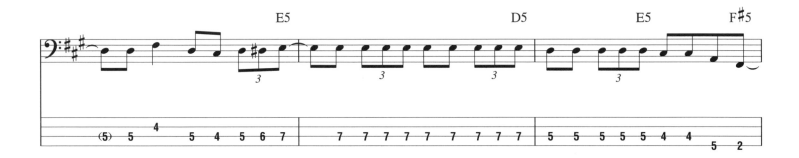

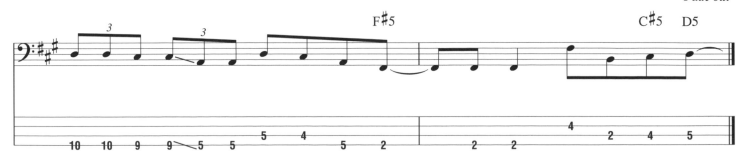

Rock of Ages

Words and Music by Joe Elliott, Richard Savage, Richard Allen, Steve Clark, Peter Willis and Robert Lange

*Composite arrangement of bass & synth. bass parts.

Drive me cra - zi - er, _____ no ser - e - nade, ___ no fire brig - ade, __ just a

Bridge

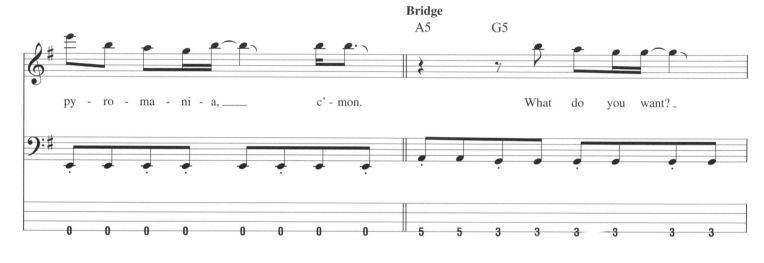

A5   G5

py - ro - ma - ni - a, ____ c' - mon.   What do you want? _

To Coda 1 ⊕

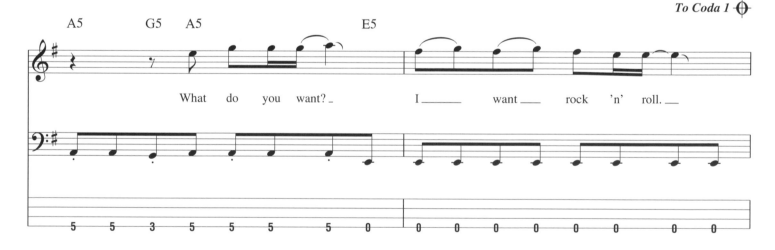

A5   G5   A5   E5

What do you want? _   I _____ want ___ rock 'n' roll. __

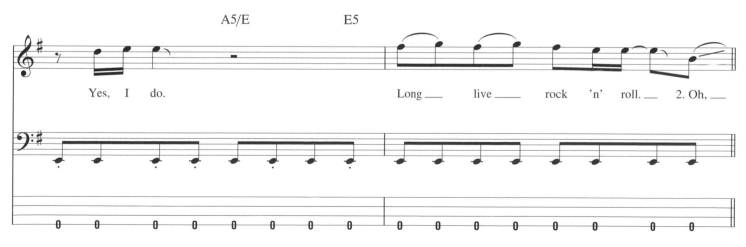

A5/E   E5

Yes, I do.   Long ___ live ___ rock 'n' roll. __ 2. Oh, __

43

Verse

let's go, let's strike a light. We're gon - na blow _ like dy - na - mite. _

I don't care _____ if it takes all _ night, gon - na set this town a - light, _ c' - mon.

Bridge

What do you want? _

What do you want? _

I _____ want _ rock 'n' roll. _ Al - right!

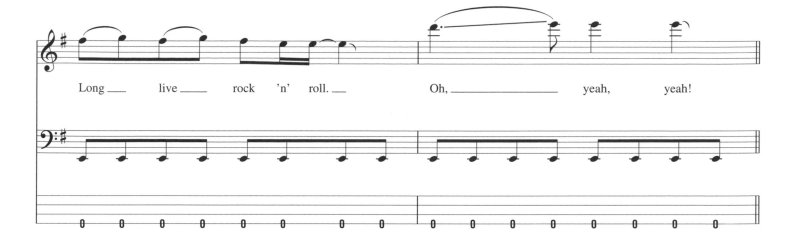

Long ___ live ___ rock 'n' roll. ___ Oh, _____ yeah, yeah!

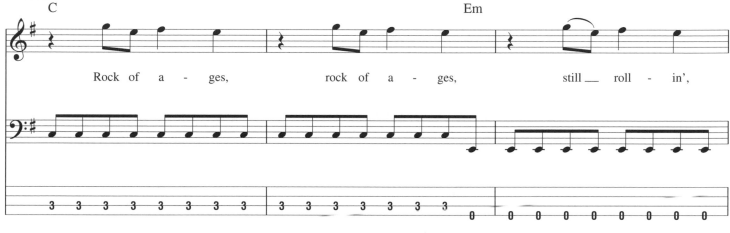

𝄋𝄋 Chorus

Rock of a - ges, rock of a - ges, still ___ roll - in',

keep a, roll - in'. Rock of a - ges, rock of a - ges,

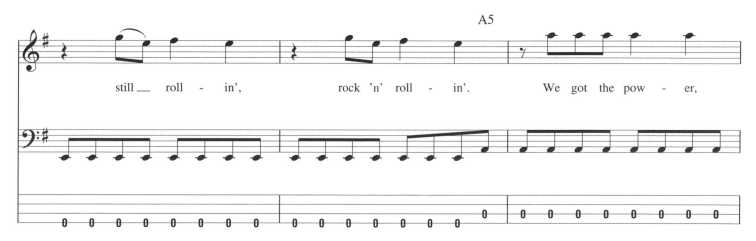

still ___ roll - in', rock 'n' roll - in'. We got the pow - er,

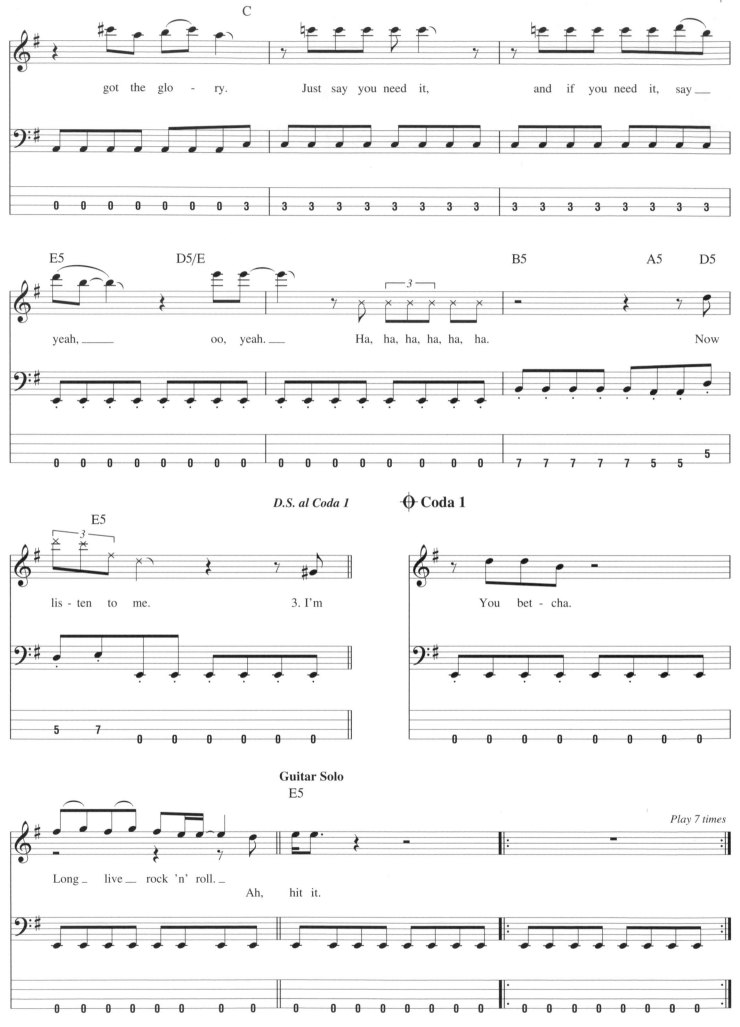

Additional Lyrics

3. I'm burnin', burnin', I got the fever.
   I know for sure there ain't no cure.
   So feel it, don't fight it, go with the flow.
   Gimme, gimme, gimme, gimme, gimme one more for the road, yeah.

Shot in the Dark

Words and Music by Ozzy Osbourne and Phil Soussan

Tune down 1/2 step:
(low to high) Eb-Ab-Db-Gb

Intro

Moderate Rock ♩ = 124

1. Out on the streets, ___ I'm stalk-ing the night, ___
2. *See additional lyrics*

on you._____ Al - right._

D.S. al Coda 1

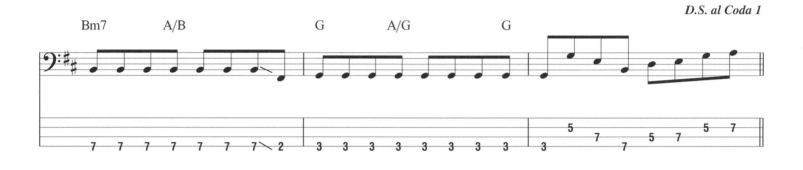

Coda 1

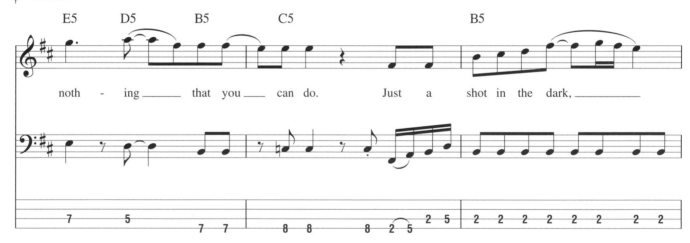

noth - ing _____ that you ___ can do.   Just a   shot in the dark, _____

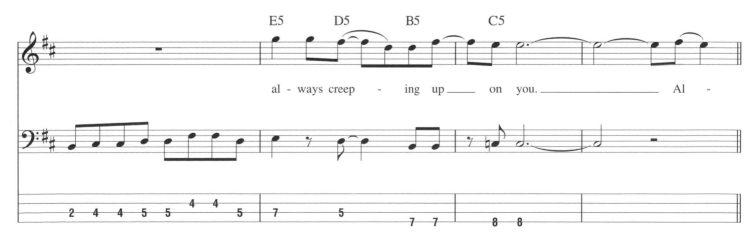

al - ways creep - ing up ____ on you. _____ Al -

Interlude

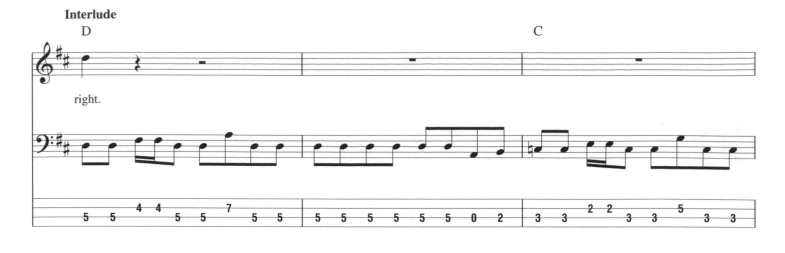

right.

Guitar Solo

D.S.S. al Coda 2

3. They're

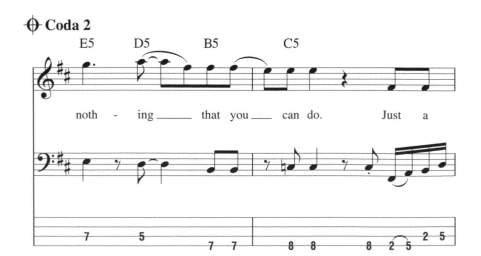

Coda 2

noth - ing _____ that you _____ can do.   Just a

52

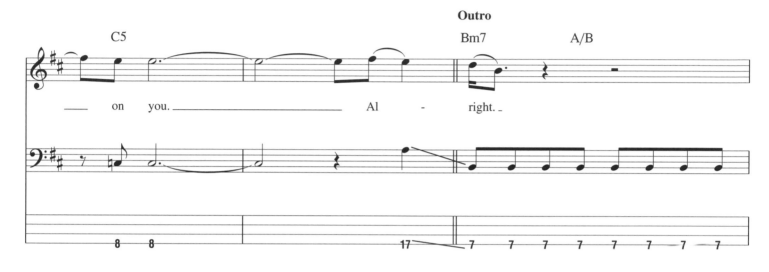

53

Additional Lyrics

2. Taught by the powers that preach over me,
   I can hear their empty reasons.
   I wouldn't listen, I learned how to fight,
   I opened up my mind to treason.

Pre-Chorus 2. But just like the wounded and when it's too late,
   They'll remember, they'll surrender.
   Never a care for the people who hate,
   Underestimate me now.

Pre-Chorus 3. They're just like the wounded and when it's too late,
   They'll remember, they'll surrender.
   Never a care for the people who hate,
   Underestimate me now.

Yankee Rose

Words by David Lee Roth
Music by Steve Vai

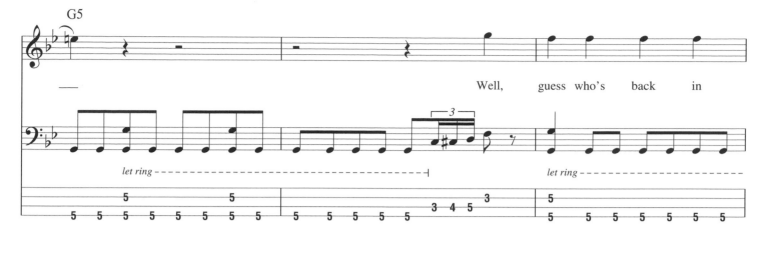

G5

Well, guess who's back in

N.C.   G7sus4

cir - cu - la - tion.   Now I don't know   what you   may have   heard, __ but what I

B♭   G5

need   right   now   is   the   o - rig - i - nal   good time   girl. _____

Pre-Chorus
Dm7

Whoa.

(She's a vi - sion from   coast   to   coast. ____   Coast   to   coast. __

57

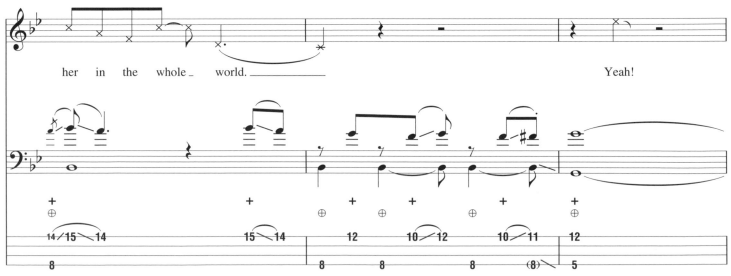

Breakdown

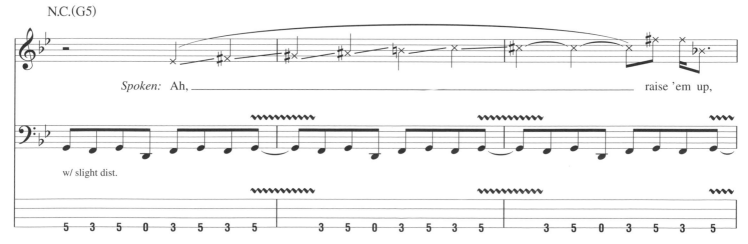

Outro

Talk Dirty to Me

Words and Music by Bobby Dall, Brett Michaels, Bruce Johannesson and Rikki Rockett

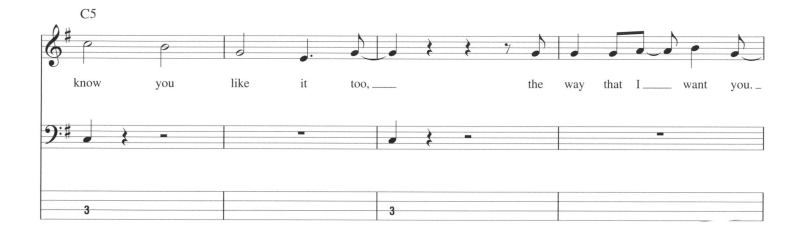

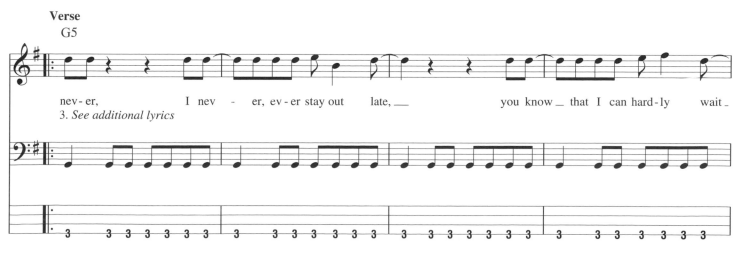

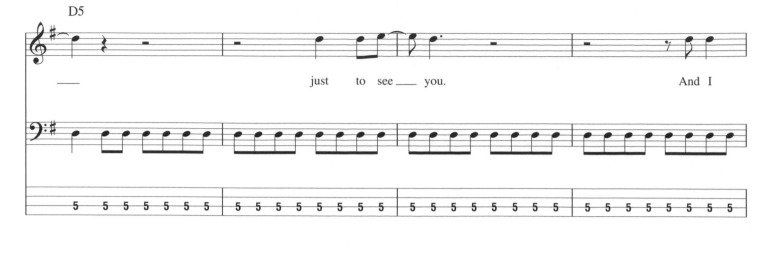

just to see ___ you.
                                    And I

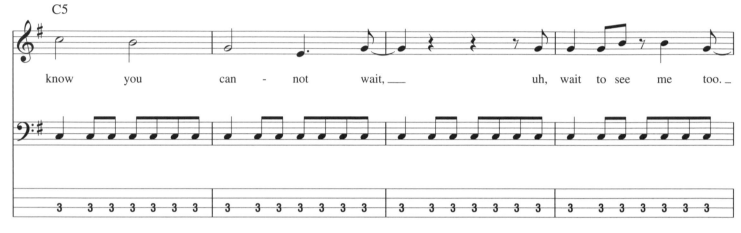

know   you   can - not   wait, ___   uh, wait   to   see   me   too. _

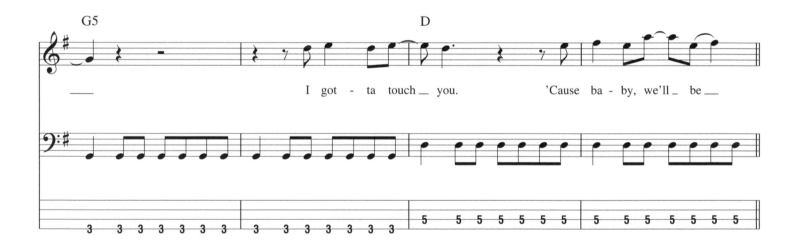

___   I   got - ta   touch ___ you.   'Cause   ba - by,   we'll _   be _

𝄋 Chorus

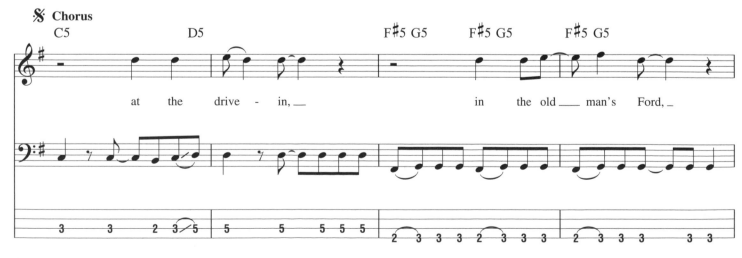

at   the   drive - in, ___   in   the   old ___ man's   Ford, _

3rd time, substitute Fill 1

{ 1., 2. be - hind the bush - es, ___   un - til I'm scream - in' for more. ___ }
{ 3. be - hind them bush - es, ___   'til I'm scream - in' for more, ___ more, more! ___ }

Down ___ the base - ment, ___ lock the cel - lar door, ___ and

To Coda ✛

ba - by, ___ talk dirt - y to me. ___   3. You know I

Fill 1

69

Additional Lyrics

3. You know I call you, I call you on the telephone,
I'm only hopin' that you're home so I can hear you
When you say those words to me and whisper so softly.
I've gotta hear you.

We're Not Gonna Take It

Words and Music by Daniel Dee Snider

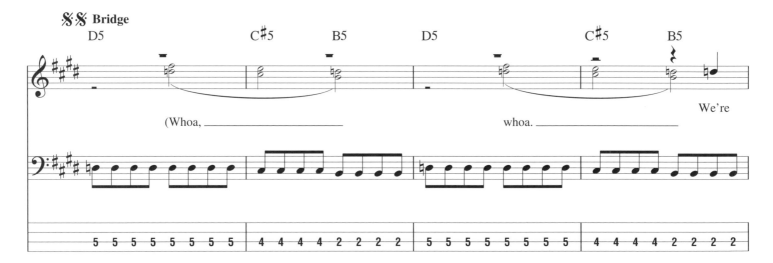

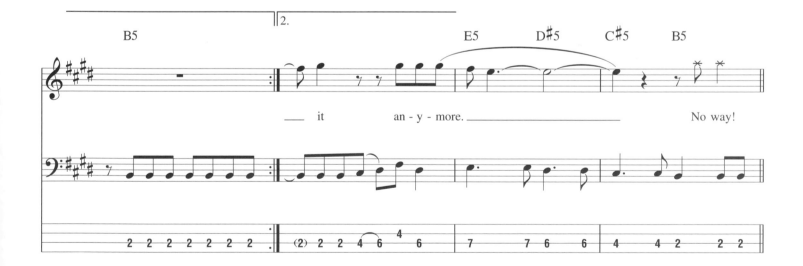

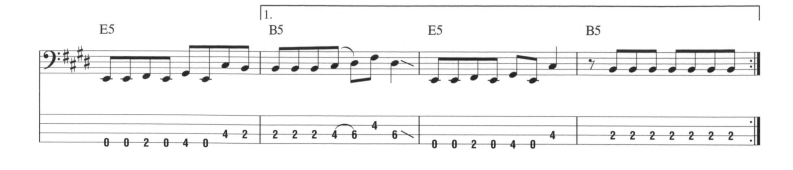

⊕ Coda 2

Breakdown-Chorus

N.C.

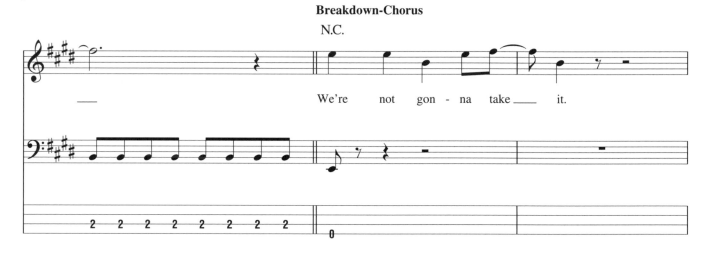

We're not gon - na take ____ it.

Bass tacet

No,   we ain't gon - na take ____ it.   We're not gon - na take ____

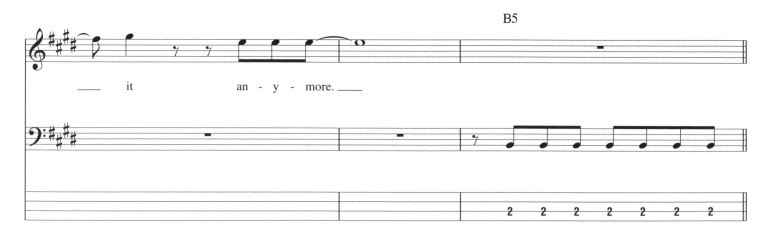

____ it   an - y - more. ____

Chorus

w/ Voc. ad lib.

2nd time, substitute Fill 1
3rd time, substitute Fill 2

We're not gon - na take ___ it. No, we ain't gon - na take ___ it.

Repeat and fade

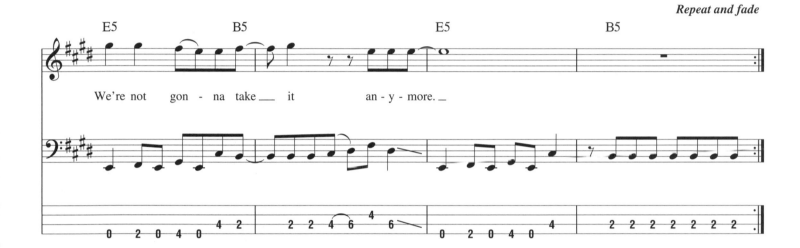

We're not gon - na take ___ it an - y - more. ___

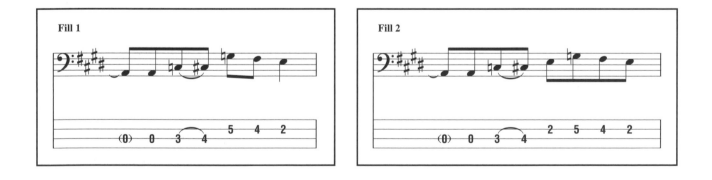

Additional Lyrics

2. Oh, you're so condescending.
   Your gall is never-ending.
   We don't want nothin'; not a thing from you.
   Your life is trite and jaded,
   Boring and confiscated.
   If that's your best, your best won't do.

HAL·LEONARD BASS PLAY·ALONG™

The Bass Play-Along Series will help you play your favorite songs quickly and easily! Just follow the tab, listen to the CD to hear how the bass should sound, and then play along using the separate backing tracks. The melody and lyrics are also included in the book in case you want to sing, or to simply help you follow along. The CD is enhanced so you can use your computer to adjust the recording to any tempo without changing pitch!

1. Rock
Songs: Another One Bites the Dust • Badge • Brown Eyed Girl • Come Together • The Joker • Low Rider • Money • Sweet Emotion.
00699674 Book/CD Pack............... $12.95

2. R&B
Songs: Get Ready • I Can't Help Myself (Sugar Pie, Honey Bunch) • I Got You (I Feel Good) • I Heard It Through the Grapevine • I Want You Back • In the Midnight Hour • My Girl • You Can't Hurry Love.
00699675 Book/CD Pack............... $12.95

3. Pop/Rock
Songs: Crazy Little Thing Called Love • Crocodile Rock • Maneater • My Life • No Reply at All • Peg • Message in a Bottle • Suffragette City.
00699677 Book/CD Pack............... $12.95

4. '90s Rock
Songs: All I Wanna Do • Fly Away • Give It Away • Hard to Handle • Jeremy • Know Your Enemy • Spiderwebs • You Oughta Know.
00699679 Book/CD Pack............... $12.95

5. Funk
Songs: Brick House • Cissy Strut • Get Off • Get Up (I Feel Like Being) a Sex Machine • Higher Ground • Le Freak • Pick up the Pieces • Super Freak.
00699680 Book/CD Pack............... $12.95

6. Classic Rock
Songs: Free Ride • Funk #49 • Gimme Three Steps • Green-Eyed Lady • Radar Love • Werewolves of London • White Room • Won't Get Fooled Again.
00699678 Book/CD Pack............... $12.95

7. Hard Rock
Songs: Crazy Train • Detroit Rock City • Iron Man • Livin' on a Prayer • Living After Midnight • Peace Sells • Smoke on the Water • The Trooper.
00699676 Book/CD Pack............... $14.95

FOR MORE INFORMATION,
SEE YOUR LOCAL MUSIC DEALER,
OR WRITE TO:

HAL·LEONARD® CORPORATION
7777 W. BLUEMOUND RD. P.O. BOX 13819
MILWAUKEE, WISCONSIN 53213

Visit Hal Leonard Online at www.halleonard.com

8. Punk Rock
Songs: Brain Stew • Buddy Holly • Dirty Little Secret • Fat Lip • Flavor of the Weak • Gotta Get Away • Lifestyles of the Rich and Famous • Man Overboard.
00699813 Book/CD Pack............... $12.95

9. Blues
Songs: All Your Love (I Miss Loving) • Born Under a Bad Sign • I'm Tore Down • I'm Your Hoochie Coochie Man • Killing Floor • Pride and Joy • Sweet Home Chicago • The Thrill Is Gone.
00699817 Book/CD Pack............... $12.95

10. Jimi Hendrix Smash Hits
Songs: All Along the Watchtower • Can You See Me? • Crosstown Traffic • Fire • Foxey Lady • Hey Joe • Manic Depression • Purple Haze • Red House • Remember • Stone Free • The Wind Cries Mary.
00699815 Book/CD Pack............... $16.95

11. Country
Songs: Achy Breaky Heart (Don't Tell My Heart) • All My Ex's Live in Texas • Boot Scootin' Boogie • Chattahoochee • Guitars, Cadillacs • I Like It, I Love It • Should've Been a Cowboy • T-R-O-U-B-L-E.
00699818 Book/CD Pack............... $12.95

13. Lennon & McCartney
Songs: All My Loving • Back in the U.S.S.R. • Day Tripper • Eight Days a Week • Get Back • I Saw Her Standing There • Nowhere Man • Paperback Writer.
00699816 .... $14.99

21. Rock Band – Modern Rock
Songs: Are You Gonna Be My Girl • Black Hole Sun • Creep • Dani California • In Bloom • Learn to Fly • Say It Ain't So • When You Were Young.
00700705 Book/CD Pack............... $14.95

22. Rock Band – Classic Rock
Songs: Ballroom Blitz • Detroit Rock City • Don't Fear the Reaper • Gimme Shelter • Highway Star • Mississippi Queen • Suffragette City • Train Kept A-Rollin'.
00700706 Book/CD Pack............... $14.95

23. Pink Floyd – Dark Side of The Moon
Songs: Any Colour You Like • Brain Damage • Breathe • Eclipse • Money • Time • Us and Them.
00700847 Book/CD Pack............... $14.99

Prices, contents, and availability subject to change without notice.
0409

Bass Recorded Versions® feature authentic transcriptions written in standard notation and tablature for bass guitar. This series features complete bass lines from the classics to contemporary superstars.

25 All-Time Rock Bass Classics
00690445 / $14.95

25 Essential Rock Bass Classics
00690210 / $15.95

Aerosmith Bass Collection
00690413 / $17.95

Best of Victor Bailey
00690718 / $19.95

Bass Tab 1990-1999
00690400 / $16.95

Bass Tab 1999-2000
00690404 / $14.95

Bass Tab White Pages
00690508 / $29.95

The Beatles Bass Lines
00690170 / $14.95

The Beatles 1962-1966
00690556 / $18.99

The Beatles 1967-1970
00690557 / $18.99

Best Bass Rock Hits
00694803 / $12.95

**Black Sabbath –
We Sold Our Soul For Rock 'N' Roll**
00660116 / $17.95

The Best of Blink 182
00690549 / $18.95

Blues Bass Classics
00690291 / $14.95

Boston Bass Collection
00690935 / $19.95

Chart Hits for Bass
00690729 / $14.95

The Best of Eric Clapton
00660187 / $19.95

Stanley Clarke Collection
00672307 / $19.95

Funk Bass Bible
00690744 / $19.95

Hard Rock Bass Bible
00690746 / $17.95

**Jimi Hendrix –
Are You Experienced?**
00690371 / $17.95

The Buddy Holly Bass Book
00660132 / $12.95

Incubus – Morning View
00690639 / $17.95

Iron Maiden Bass Anthology
00690867 / $22.99

Best of Kiss for Bass
00690080 / $19.95

Bob Marley Bass Collection
00690568 / $19.95

Best of Marcus Miller
00690811 / $19.99

Motown Bass Classics
00690253 / $14.95

Mudvayne – Lost & Found
00690798 / $19.95

Nirvana Bass Collection
00690066 / $19.95

No Doubt – Tragic Kingdom
00120112 / $22.95

The Offspring – Greatest Hits
00690809 / $17.95

**Jaco Pastorius –
Greatest Jazz Fusion Bass Player**
00690421 / $17.95

The Essential Jaco Pastorius
00690420 / $18.95

Pearl Jam – Ten
00694882 / $14.95

Pink Floyd – Dark Side of the Moon
00660172 / $14.95

The Best of Police
00660207 / $14.95

Pop/Rock Bass Bible
00690747 / $17.95

Queen – The Bass Collection
00690065 / $17.95

R&B Bass Bible
00690745 / $17.95

Rage Against the Machine
00690248 / $16.95

The Best of Red Hot Chili Peppers
00695285 / $24.95

**Red Hot Chili Peppers –
Blood Sugar Sex Magik**
00690064 / $19.95

**Red Hot Chili Peppers –
By the Way**
00690585 / $19.95

**Red Hot Chili Peppers –
Californication**
00690390 / $19.95

**Red Hot Chili Peppers –
Greatest Hits**
00690675 / $18.95

**Red Hot Chili Peppers –
One Hot Minute**
00690091 / $18.95

**Red Hot Chili Peppers –
Stadium Arcadium**
00690853 / $24.95

**Red Hot Chili Peppers –
Stadium Arcadium: Deluxe Edition**
Book/2-CD Pack
00690863 / $39.95

Rock Bass Bible
00690446 / $19.95

Rolling Stones
00690256 / $16.95

System of a Down – Toxicity
00690592 / $19.95

Top Hits for Bass
00690677 / $14.95

**Stevie Ray Vaughan –
Lightnin' Blues 1983-1987**
00694778 / $19.95

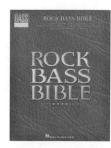

0309

BASS BUILDERS

A series of technique book/audio packages created for the purposeful building and development of your chops. Each volume is written by an expert in that particular technique. And with the inclusion of audio, the added dimension of hearing exactly how to play particular grooves and techniques make this truly like a private lesson. The added use of photos makes the lessons complete!

BASS FITNESS – AN EXERCISING HANDBOOK
by Josquin des Prés
INCLUDES TAB
00660177 ....$9.95

BASS FOR BEGINNERS
THE COMPLETE GUIDE
by Glenn Letsch
INCLUDES TAB
00695099 Book/CD Pack.....................$19.95

BASS IMPROVISATION
by Ed Friedland
INCLUDES TAB
00695164 Book/CD Pack.....................$17.95

BLUES BASS
by Jon Liebman
INCLUDES TAB
00695235 Book/CD Pack.....................$19.95

BUILDING ROCK BASS LINES
by Ed Friedland
00695692 Book/CD Pack.....................$17.95

BUILDING WALKING BASS LINES
by Ed Friedland
00695008 Book/CD Pack.....................$19.95

RON CARTER – BUILDING JAZZ BASS LINES
00841240 Book/CD Pack.....................$19.95

DICTIONARY OF BASS GROOVES
by Sean Malone
INCLUDES TAB
00695266 Book/CD Pack.....................$14.95

EXPANDING WALKING BASS LINES
by Ed Friedland
00695026 Book/CD Pack.....................$19.95

FINGERBOARD HARMONY FOR BASS
by Gary Willis
00695043 Book/CD Pack.....................$17.95

FUNK BASS
by Jon Liebman
INCLUDES TAB
00699348 Book/CD Pack.....................$19.95

FUNK/FUSION BASS
by Jon Liebman
INCLUDES TAB
00696553 Book/CD Pack.....................$19.95

HIP-HOP BASS
101 GROOVES, RIFFS, LOOPS, AND BEATS
by Josquin des Prés
INCLUDES TAB
00695589 Book/CD Pack.....................$14.95

JAZZ BASS
by Ed Friedland
00695084 Book/CD Pack.....................$17.95

JERRY JEMMOTT – BLUES AND RHYTHM & BLUES BASS TECHNIQUE
INCLUDES TAB
00695176 Book/CD Pack.....................$17.95

JUMP 'N' BLUES BASS
by Keith Rosier
INCLUDES TAB
00695292 Book/CD Pack.....................$16.95

THE LOST ART OF COUNTRY BASS
AN INSIDE LOOK AT COUNTRY BASS FOR ELECTRIC AND UPRIGHT PLAYERS
by Keith Rosier
INCLUDES TAB
00695107 Book/CD Pack.....................$19.95

REGGAE BASS
by Ed Friedland
INCLUDES TAB
00695163 Book/CD Pack.....................$16.95

ROCK BASS
by Jon Liebman
INCLUDES TAB
00695083 Book/CD Pack.....................$17.95

'70S FUNK & DISCO BASS
101 GROOVIN' BASS PATTERNS
by Josquin des Prés
INCLUDES TAB
00695614 Book/CD Pack.....................$14.95

SIMPLIFIED SIGHT-READING FOR BASS
by Josquin des Prés
INCLUDES TAB
00695085 Book/CD Pack.....................$17.95

6-STRING BASSICS
by David Gross
INCLUDES TAB
00695221 Book/CD Pack.....................$12.95

SLAP BASS ESSENTIALS
by Josquin dés Pres and Bunny Brunel
INCLUDES TAB
00696563 Book/CD Pack.....................$19.95

WORLD BEAT GROOVES FOR BASS
by Tony Cimorosi
INCLUDES TAB
00695335 Book/CD Pack.....................$14.95

FOR MORE INFORMATION, SEE YOUR LOCAL MUSIC DEALER, OR WRITE TO:

HAL•LEONARD®
CORPORATION
7777 W. BLUEMOUND RD. P.O. BOX 13819 MILWAUKEE, WI 53213

Visit Hal Leonard Online at **www.halleonard.com**

Prices, contents and availability subject to change without notice; All prices are listed in U.S. funds